THE WARRIOR ON BENDED KNEES

Inspired Writings
By
Sandra J Yearman

SERAPHIM PUBLISHING LLC

WE WILL BRING LIGHT TO ALL THE DARK PLACES

Registered trademark-
Sandra J Yearman
Seraphim Publishing
438 Water St. Cambridge, WI 53523

Copyright © 2008 Sandra J Yearman
Produced in the United States of America
Author : Sandra J Yearman
Editor: Sandra J Yearman
Cover Design by Sandra J Yearman
Layout and design by Sandra J Yearman

All rights reserved. No part of this book may be reproduced, stored in or introduced into a retrieval system, or transmitted, in any form or by any means, electronic or mechanical, including photocopying or recording or otherwise copied for public or private use—other than for "fair use" as brief quotations embodied in articles and reviews--without written permission from the author.

Library of Congress Control Number: 2009906240
ISBN: 978-0-9815791-5-3
First Edition

To All God's Holy Warriors
Who On Bended Knees Do Pray
To God In All His Glory
'Help Mankind Find A Better Way'
Amen
Amen
Amen

CONTENTS

DEDICATION

Man's Blood Soaked Battle Fields..........................7
Warriors Are Called Forth................................11
A Voice Called Moses 14
The Temple Of Jesus......................................18
The Lord Of Hosts..21
Jesus Walk Among Us 23
A Holy Warrior Rides 26
Water The Gardens Of Our Minds...........................30
Judgment...33

SEEKING LIGHT IN THE DARKNESS

This World Is But A Testing Ground 35
Choices...38
Dark Ways...40
Cleanse This House................................42
Shadows In The Night..............................44
As We Stumble Through These Dark Worlds....46
When You Are Drowning In The Darkness........50
A Light In The Darkness...........................52

CONTENTS

Are We The Parents Of The Earth......................55
The Trumpets Of War...59
When Is An Angel's Voice Muffled....................63
An Angel's Heart...67
The Warrior Weeps..69
Demons In The Night 72
Where Did The Thunder Go..............................74

COMING HOME

Before Darkness I Will Stand 77
The Living Flame..79
Angel Of Mercy...81
God Of All The Heavens......................................83
As Illusions End..85
Arms On The Cross..87
The Morning Star...89
The Warriors Among Us.....................................91
As The Walls Of Hell Were Broken....................93
The Time Of Angels Is At Hand.........................97

5

Dedication

Man's Blood Soaked Battle Fields

This world is but a battle field
We are so long from Home
Lord shield us and protect us
With You we are never alone

God with arms wide open
Shields us from the night
He welcomes all His children
And stands before our plight

We are attacked by darkness
Lord please dissolve our fears
Increase our faith with blessings
And always hold us near

God with arms wide open
Shields us from the night
He welcomes all His children
And stands before our plight

The warrior in his holiness
On bended knee does pray
'Lord carry me in battle'
'Lord find a better way'

God with arms wide open
Shields us from the night
He welcomes all His children
And stands before our plight

If God is Love and Mercy
Where did His children stray
God forgive us for our darkness
And create a brighter day

God with arms wide open
Shields us from the night
He welcomes all His children
And stands before our plight

Where man's blood soaked
battle fields
A tribute to our darkest ways
And the tremendous weapons that we
wield
Are but a memory of far-gone unholy
days

God with arms wide open
Shields us from the night
He welcomes all His children
And stands before our plight

Where the red blood flowed like rivers
And where destruction became king
Lord let Heaven's gardens flower
Lord let Your Holy Name now ring

Amen Amen Amen

Warriors Are Called Forth

Who heals the warriors
Those who protect our world
Those who face horror
Those who help the victims

So that others will be free and safe

Who heals their wounds
Who carries them when they have fallen
Who remembers the heroes

The warriors are called forth to fight
On battle grounds soaked with blood

But who nourishes them when they are weak
Who picks up the splintered pieces of their bodies and spirits

When they are the casualties
And every one of us is a casualty of war

Who helps them distinguish between the nightmares and life
Often they are betrayed by those in power
They are forgotten by those they protected
They are ridiculed by ignorance

God please help this world to remember
That every warrior is someone's child

God please teach this world
That people are not disposable

God please heal and carry the warriors
of this world

God send Your Angels, Your warriors
To protect them on the battle fields
To comfort them and to dry their tears
To give them faith and to protect them
from the darkness

God Bless the service men and women
The police officers, the firemen and
All those who protect us

Amen Amen Amen

Voice Called Moses

A Voice called down from Heaven
'Moses take my Hand'
'And lead my precious children'
'Out of pharaoh's land'

Moses said 'my Savior'
'I will take a stand'
'And I will lead Your children'
'To Your promised land'

Moses stood before darkness
Moses took a stand
And Moses freed God's children
As was the Holy plan

A Voice called down from Heaven
'Moses take my Hand'
'And lead my precious children'
'Out of pharaoh's land'

Moses had no weapons
He had the shield of faith
He wielded the rod and staff of God
He was consumed with Holy Grace

Pharaoh's army followed
Their fates to them unknown
And to all His children
God's mighty power was shown

Fear had overtaken
The blessed children of Israel
As they fled the vicious army
That would take them back to hell

A Voice called down from Heaven
'Moses take my Hand'
'And lead my precious children'
'Out of pharaoh's land'

The waters they were parted
The mighty seas were stilled
And Moses led God's children
As the Loving God had willed

Pharaoh's army followed
God's children they would enslave
But God's power was almighty
And all God's children were saved

The promises of Heaven
And the blessings from above
Were showered on the children
As well as Grace and Love

God in all His Glory
And Heaven with all its might
Rescued His children from darkness
And stood before their plight

A Voice called down from Heaven
'Moses take my Hand'
'And lead my precious children'
'Out of pharaoh's land'

Amen Amen Amen

The Temple Of Jesus

The temple of Jesus
The Son and the Lamb
The Bright Morning Star
The Great I Am

The Brilliance of Heaven
A Gift from above
The Word and the Song
And a warrior of Love

A Savior and Servant
An Author and King
The Lord of the Hosts
Of whom Angels sing

The Bridegroom and Prophet
The Rock and the Way
The Door and the Key
Man's debt He did pay

The Messiah and Shepherd
The Prince of all creation
The Teacher and Day Spring
The King of all nations

The Bread and the Wine
The Breath and the Soul
The Father and Son
The Spirit as told

The One and the Three
Eternal and forgiving
The Fountain of Life
The Breath of the living

The Star of the night
The Jewel of the Heavens
The Lord and Creator
Of all God has given

The King of all Kings
The Begotten Son
The Father of Jesus
Our souls He won

And through the ages
May His Holy Name ring
Immanuel
Our Savior and King

Amen Amen Amen

The Lord Of Hosts

The Lord of Hosts, My Savior and Redeemer
Please forgive me and cleanse the iniquities of this dark world

Consume me with the Holy Spirit of the Heavens
Carry me that I may find my true purpose in this world

Ignite within me the flame of Holy faith
And keep the flame alive with the Living Fire

Fill me with the Song of the Heavens
That my heart may sing with joy

Lead me down the path of the Angels
And help me to hear Your Holy Voice

Let the Flame of the Lord of Hosts
Saturate these dark worlds and turn
night into day

Help me to find my way back to You

Amen Amen Amen

Jesus Walk Among Us

Jesus walk among us
In this madness we create
Our death march of destruction
Fueled by our fears, fed by our hate

Jesus walk among us
In these unholy battle fields
Give us strength and purpose
Help us not to yield

To the terror and the horror
That obliterates the Son
To the prejudice and sorrow
To the deadly game we run

Jesus walk among us
In this battle field
Protect us and surround us
Your Holy sword to wield

Jesus walk among us
Your Light in us create
Save us from our demons
Redeem us from our hate

Protect us from this madness
This war of hopelessness and despair
Free us from our bondage
Carry us out of death's dark lair

Jesus walk among us
Your sacrifice, did cleanse
Your blood washed our darkness
Your Love, God did send

Jesus walk among us
Your Presence we will know
We will feel the warmth of Your Love
And Your Holy Light will show

Jesus walk among us
Save us from the dead
Redeem us with Your Mercy
As Your Holy words were said

Jesus walk among us

Amen Amen Amen

A Holy Warrior Rides

God sent forth an army
This world has never seen
An army without rest
Led by a Holy King

The army marched to the song of faith
The strongest power known
God carried them in battle
God carried them to their Heavenly Home

God in all His Holiness
And Heaven with all its Might
Stood before a dying world
And darkness lost the fight

Great armies they defeated
The dark fortresses could not stand
Before the Spirit of the Lord
And the Holiest King in all the land

In His understanding
God blessed this holy man
Who fought with faith and courage
And love songs to God he sang

God in all His Holiness
And Heaven with all its Might
Stood before a dying world
And darkness lost the fight

The army rode for justice
The army took a stand
To save the world from darkness
Every woman, child and man

The banner they rode under
The shield that stood before
God blessed them and saved them
And His Holy army soared

God in all His Holiness
And Heaven with all its Might
Stood before a dying world
And darkness lost the fight

The child king defeated giants
Because he surrendered to his Lord
His body had no boundaries
His holy spirit soared

The Angels heralded the coming
The demons fought with all their might
The Song of God poured forth
Bringing Heaven's Holy Light

God in all His Holiness
And Heaven with all its Might
Stood before a dying world
And darkness lost the fight

In these days of turmoil
In these days of strife
The strongest weapon we can have
Is God within our life

The Holiest of warriors
Prevails unto this day
The Holy Angels of the Lord
Will help make a better Way

Amen Amen Amen

Water The Gardens Of Our Minds

God gave man a garden
Filled with all the blessings
That only God could create
Blessings that were Heaven sent

God gave man charge over these blessings
Over His creations
To protect
To nourish
To bless
For God is Love

And man, who does not recognize
His true place in these worlds

And man, who does not recognize
The Holy tests of God

And man who calls darkness
Upon himself

Turns around the words of God
And uses them to commit great acts of violence
To justify the victimization of God's creations
To destroy the blessings
That God has given us

If life in these worlds is a testing ground
If mans test is to overcome darkness
And to choose Holiness
As Jesus showed us with His life

Then, what has mankind shown himself and Heaven

Would we say, 'God, give us easier tests because we are failing the ones You have sent us'

Or would we say, 'God, consume us with the Holy Spirit and give us what we need to awaken in these dark worlds'

The choices are ours...

Lord God, bless Your children
Help us to overcome the darkness
Guide our choices
And bring us Home

Amen Amen Amen

Judgment

If God is with us always
How can there be a judgment day

If you keep God out of your life
Do you fear a time when
He will arrive and judge you

But, if you ask God
To fill you with the Holy Spirit
To guide you

To carry you
To be with you always
What is there to fear...

God let Thy Will be done

Amen Amen Amen

Seeking Light In The Darkness

This World Is But A Testing Ground

This world is but a testing ground
Life's obstacles test our faith
Trials of forgiveness and courage
Choices between darkness and Grace

Lord lead Your flock to freedom
Lord create a brighter day
Lord save us from our darkness
Lord that in Your Holiness we may

Remember we are Your children
Remember why we are here
We praise the Lord Almighty
We call Your Spirit near

This world is but a testing ground
Life's obstacles test our faith
Trials of forgiveness and courage
Choices between darkness and Grace

As my enemies gather
And darkness attempts to block the Son
My Lord prepares a table before me
A battle He has won

My destiny is in Your Hands
I kneel before Your Throne
I choose the path of Righteousness
I will never walk alone

This world is but a testing ground
Life's obstacles test our faith
Trials of forgiveness and courage
Choices between darkness and Grace

Lord help me to always
Hear Your Voice in the darkness
And on Your Holy Path I will stay

Amen Amen Amen

Choices

How do we understand our roles here
If we do not understand who we are

How do we determine our true
purpose here
If we do not seek the truth

The choices are ours
To sculpture our beings
To impact this world
To be of significance

We define ourselves by our fears

We outline our caricatures by
The limits we establish

We cloak ourselves because

We are afraid to be a light in the darkness

God we seek the Truth
Bless us with the answers
Calm our fears

Amen Amen Amen

Dark Ways

When the way is too dark
Instead of turning in fear
Ask God to send His Light
And to hold you near

When the roar of chaos, deafens your ears
When the noise overwhelms you
And fills you with fear
Pray that it is only God's Voice that you hear

When you are afraid of the sounds in the night
The fear overwhelms you
The horror and fright
Ask God to protect you with Heavens Holy Might

When the sounds of dying
Are all around
The music seems dead
You hear no other sound

Ask God to send you
The Song that pours forth
The music of Heaven
The Song that opens Heaven's door

Amen Amen Amen

Cleanse This House

Cleanse this house from darkness
Protect us in the storm
Guide our every movement
Carry us as we roam

Help us as we wander
Show us as You see
Bless us with Your Mercy
Let this journey be

A powerful adventure
A journey told of old
The Holy rite of passage
A warrior it would mold

Blessed are all the wanderers
When Your Truth they do seek
Blessed are all creation
When Your Holy Name, they speak

When the trials are conquered
And through the tests we grow
And realize the answers
The wanderers journey Home

Amen Amen Amen

Shadows In The Night

What would we kill for
Why would we sin
The calling of darkness
Again and again

It is for power that we barter
It is for greed that we fight
It is for fear that man calls
To the shadows in the night

Hell's legions march
As mans darkness calls them forth
Why do we seek hell
Instead of the Source

God is the Power
God is the King
God is the Source
Of whom Angels sing

God of all Heavens
God of all Might
God of all Glory
Heaven's true Light

No darkness can stand
Before the power of the Light
Why does man call
To the shadows in the night

Amen Amen Amen

As We Stumble Through These Dark Worlds

Who will stand when others falter
Who will wipe away the tears
Who will stand up to the darkness
Who will overcome our fears

The warriors that God sends us
His Angels hold us near
This world is but a testing ground
And our lives are simply mirrors

Of the holiness within us
Of the demons that we call
Are we only shattered pieces
Can we escape our prison walls

God will send His Angels
To guide us through these tests
They pray that we will listen
They pray that God will bless

As we stumble through these dark worlds
And cry out in our pain
Perhaps these obstacles are challenges
Our holiness to gain

Our lives are but mazes
In these worlds of guilt and sin
The goal is to find the path
To return to where we begin

God will send His Angels
To guide us through these tests
They pray that we will listen
They pray that God will bless

The test is to overcome the darkness
The burdens and the sins
To rise above the chaos
To conquer and to win

Our darkness builds obstacles
That block us from His Face
We must pray to overcome them
To inherit Holy Grace

God will send His Angels
To guide us through these tests
They pray that we will listen
They pray that God will bless

For Heaven in its Holiness
And God the One in Three
Are aware of all our acts
Our thoughts, our words our deeds

God awaken within us
The Holiness of Your Sight
That we may overcome the darkness
And find You in the night

And God will send His Angels
To guide us through these tests
They pray that we will listen
They pray that God will bless

Amen Amen Amen

When You Are Drowning In The Darkness

When screams disturb your nightmares
And it is your own voice that you hear
When you are drowning in the darkness
When you are overcome with fear

The Lord will always help you
The Lord will be at hand
Ask that He will save you
Ask for Him to stand

Before you in the darkness
To wipe away your tears
To lift you from the chaos
To bring His Angels near

When your screams are muffled
Because you walk with the dead
When your life source is without you
Yet the nightmares have no end

Call upon God's Holiness
Call upon God's Grace
Ask that He will save you
From the awful place

That your mind has created
That your body fed
The choices that led you
To walk among the dead

Amen Amen Amen

A Light In The Darkness

Darkness shrieks with horror
As Heaven takes a stand
God's Holy army
Reclaims Heaven's Holy lands

And the death masks of terror
Are ground into sand
As God's Holy army
Reclaims Heaven's Holy lands

All of God's creatures
Will learn to take a stand
To help God's Holy army
Reclaim God's Holy lands

The demons that dwell with us
And the darkness in our souls
Will be cleansed by God's Holy Light
And we will break hells' horrific hold

All of God's creatures
In all the worlds that ever were
Will rise above the chaos
Will follow the Heavenly star

And the voice that cries from the darkness
For Justice and for Grace
Will help God's Holy army
Save God's Holy places

As God's creation
Learn to let go of their fear
The paths will be illuminated
They will realize that Holiness is near

As God's Holy army
Fights against the night
We pray that God will bless us
With His Holy Sight

That we may see the obstacles
That we have put in place
To imprison and to trap us
To keep us from His Grace

Lord bless us with Your Mercy
Fill us with Your Love
We pray that God's Holy army
Stands before us; from above

Save us from the demons
Tear the high places down
Bring us back to Heaven
We believe in the Trinity's Holy Crown

Amen Amen Amen

Are We Parents Of The Earth

God gave man dominion over this
earth
Do we understand the extent
Do we understand the true meaning
Do we understand what He meant

Are we our brothers keeper
Are we parents of this earth
Is this a Holy blessing
Why then, do we treat it like a curse

Will we continue to destroy creation
For profit and for gain
Do we seek the Face of Heaven
Or create worlds of terror, horror and
pain

If you looked at every creature
Like your daughter or your son
Would you fill this world with darkness
Which our fear and ignorance have begun

To destroy all God's Holy blessings
To create a world filled with disgrace
To allow the demons to devour
To turn this garden into waste

Will we continue to destroy creation
For profit and for gain
Do we seek the Face of Heaven
Or create worlds of terror, horror and pain

Every life force God created
Is a miracle unique
Do we tend to all God's children
Do we listen when He speaks

Do we honor one another
His commandments do we keep
Do we seek the Face of Heaven
Or in darkness do we weep

Will we continue to destroy creation
For profit and for gain
Do we seek the Face of Heaven
Or create worlds of terror, horror and pain

The choice is ours you understand
In all we seek and do
Why then, do we choose death
When to God we could be true

We have the power to change
All which we do not like
Heaven is waiting for us
Yet we are lost within the night

Will we continue to destroy creation
For profit and for gain
Do we seek the Face of Heaven
Or create worlds of terror, horror and pain

Forgive us Lord of Mercy
Help us in our plight
Stand before and heal us
Save us from the night

Amen Amen Amen

The Trumpets Of War

The trumpets of war herald
That death is at the door
The forces of darkness surround us
In this holy war

And God's Holy army
Through the Heavens soar
To stand before creation
In this holy war

Hordes of demons attack us
They pierce us with their fear
They fight without honor
The battle wages near

Each of us is tested
To stand up and to face
Darkness at our threshold
Darkness in this place

And God's Holy army
Through the Heavens soar
To stand before creation
In this holy war

The test is more than courage
The test is that of faith
Do we surrender and fall
Or in God's Holy army take our place

This life is but a testing ground
And death is at our door
If we conquer and succeed
Then in Heaven we will soar

And God's Holy army
Through the Heavens soar
To stand before creation
In this holy war

As the battle wages
As we are torn by war
As we are tested by our choices
To whom do we open the door

The trumpets herald victory
God's Holy army takes the night
And stands before creation
And saves us from our plight

And God's Holy army
Through the Heavens soar
To stand before creation
In this holy war

The warrior in his holiness
On bended knee does pray
'Lord carry me in battle'
'Lord make a better Way'

'bring Light into these dark worlds'
'guide us in these tests'
'fill us with Your Spirit'
'and creation may You Bless'

Amen Amen Amen

When Is An Angels Voice Muffled

When did God get lost in the shuffle
When did we become ashamed to pray
When is an Angel's voice muffled
When did darkness dictate the way

When did our priorities become morbid
When did our children lose their way
When did Holiness take a backseat
When did we forget how to pray

Our nation was surrendered to God
Now we are afraid to mention His Name
For fear a demon will sue us
How did this happen? Who do we blame?

We worship greed and power
Our pockets we do line
With the blood and sweat of others
We forget the words of the divine

The victims without voices
The children we have sold
The nameless and the homeless
Are all God's children we were told

Nature in all its glory
Was also Heaven sent
For us to tend and nurture
Not to ravage and neglect

We call the horror upon us
We terrorize ourselves
We fear and hate our neighbors
Among us demons dwell

We neglect those who need us
We turn away those with pain
We glorify the soulless
What have the children of God to gain

Upon this road of darkness
This trail of horror and tears
Do we not remember Heaven
Have we forgotten how to call God near

Lord lift these death masks from us
Restore our Holy souls
Awaken us from darkness
Forgive our unholy goals

Blow life back into the victims
Heal what we have destroyed
Remove the demons from us
Cleanse what we have soiled

Remind us we are Your children
Bring us to Your Grace
Let us hear the Voice of Heaven
Let us seek Your Holy Face

Amen Amen Amen

An Angels Heart

Lord give me strength and courage
To say what must be said
To stand before creation
And darkness not to wed

Lord give me love and compassion
And never let me turn away
From the victims and the needy
Heavenly Father, make a better Way

Lord give me wisdom and a Holy heart
That I may not judge and condemn
Fill me with Your Justice
And help me to take a stand

That I may face the darkness
And say 'no further shall you go'
'you are no longer wanted'
'your chaos will not grow'

'you will not conquer this world'
For death has lost its fear
Because a voice cried from the darkness
And called the Heavens near

Amen Amen Amen

The Warrior Weeps

The warrior weeps with Holy passion
As darkness takes its tolls
Tears cried with compassion
For creations fragile souls

The ransom of creation
Was paid with Holy blood
Holy warriors were sent
With God's eternal Love

Darkness stalks creation
There is terror in the night
Blood on the hands of demons
Voices cry with fright

The ransom of creation
Was paid with Holy blood
Holy warriors were sent
With God's eternal Love

The scales of life must balance
As covenants are betrayed
The justice of law and mercy
Our crosses we display

The ransom of creation
Was paid with Holy blood
Holy warriors were sent
With God's eternal Love

Shadows hide the faces
Of demons wearing human masks
To conquer these obstacles
Is creation's holy task

The ransom of creation
Was paid with Holy blood
Holy warriors were sent
With God's eternal Love

Holy men unit
Their prayer, power beyond belief
Summoning the Heavens
Healing creation's grief

The ransom of creation
Was paid with Holy blood
Holy warriors were sent
With God's eternal Love

Amen Amen Amen

Demons In The Night

The sins of the fathers
The blood of the sons
A journey of darkness
That is never won

Stopping the darkness
Within and without
The frailty of man
A world filled with doubt

Whom do we turn to
To see through the night
The kings of men
Encourage our plight

Mutilated by darkness
Our forms no longer to recognize
Blinded by deception
Numb to the cries

Who is the demon
Who represents the light
In this ancient of battles
Fought with man's might

The choice is forever
The choice that was of old
The King of the Heavens
Or the kings of a world gone cold

Amen Amen Amen

Where Did The Thunder Go

In all the worlds that ever were
There were rituals of great significance
Rites of passage
Confirmation

Rites that determined leadership
Rites that signified manhood
Rites that proved ownership
Rites that lead to holiness

Songs were sung
Honors were bestowed
Destines were determined

Where are these rites today

How do you understand your
substance
If you are afraid to be challenged

How do you know you are a winner
If you never enter the race

How do you conquer darkness
If you are afraid to face your fears

What do we become if we hide from
the tests
What do we become if we shriek with
fear

What are we becoming
Lord God, give us what we need to
conquer
The darkest regions

Amen Amen Amen

Coming Home

Before Darkness I Will Stand

God help me to overcome the frailties
of humanity
Help me to overcome the limits of
time and space
Help me to awaken
Allow me to seek Your Holy Face

The boundaries of our bodies
The limits of our minds
The fears that inhibit us
The guilt and sin that binds

Us to these worlds of darkness
To these places of disgrace
Lord help my spirit to transcend
Allow me to seek Your Holy Face

The power is within us
Our choices they decree
The paths that we will take
I choose the path to Thee

The answers are so simple
Faith and Forgiveness are the
Holy keys
To overcome the darkness
I will pray upon my knees

That God will give me guidance
And put into my hand
The Holy torch of Heaven
Before darkness I will stand

Amen Amen Amen

The Living Flame

Christ Face and Three
Hand of the Lord
I will know my God
I will carry the sword

Of faith eternal
Of fire and forgiveness
Heaven awaits me
The One who is blameless

Christ Face and Three
Awaken from dreams
Saved from the nightmares
Healed from the screams

Hand of the Lord
This I will see
When I awaken
And walk with Thee

Amen Amen Amen

Angel of Mercy

Angel of mercy
Sent from above
Please stand before us
Angel of love

Shelter and guide us
Protect us and heal
Carry and save us
Show us what is real

Angel of mercy
Sent from above
Helper of God
Spirit and dove

Angel of mercy
Show us the way
Open our hearts
Teach us to pray

And when I see you
I know I will stay
With God forever
And ever, I pray

Amen Amen Amen

God Of All The Heavens

God of all the Heavens
Savior of all worlds without end
Lord of all creation
Father of all men

Near to You, we desire
We ask to see Your Face
Fill us with Your Fire
Bless us with Your Grace

Engulf us with Your Presence
Free us from this place
Speak that we may hear You
Our sins, may You erase

Ignite us with Your passion
Redeem us with Your Son
Carry us to Heaven
When this journey is done

Amen Amen Amen

As Illusions End

When dreams that were so distant
Away from us do flee
And the dreams of this existence
Our eyes no longer see

When memories have forsaken
The frailties of the flesh
When sleep calms the chaos
Slumber without distress

When life with all its beauty
And life with all its pain
Changes our existence
And we come Home again

When Heaven's doors are opened
And Light shows us the Way
Our Heavenly Father is waiting
Our Home with Him to stay

When His Voice is calling
And Angels on their wings
The soul has found release
And Heavenward does sing

Amen Amen Amen

Arms On The Cross

Arms on the cross
That shield and protect us
Our Savior's Love
That saved and redeemed us

Angels wings
That shelter and guide
God's Holy Voice
From which no man can hide

Eternal and always
In Spirit and in Light
Stands before His children
And stops the terror in the night

With Justice and with Mercy
Prophets had fore told
Of a Love so Holy
That it would break the darkest hold

Blood of the Savior
Manna of life
Redeemer of all children
Father of life

Arms on the cross
That shield and protect us
Our Savior's Love
That saved and redeemed us

Amen Amen Amen

The Morning Star

The star in the east
That tears down the night
The star in the east
That dissolves mans fright

And in the morning
A star you will see
That God sent to man
A blessing from Three

A King with no equal
A King on bended knee
The power of Heaven
The Love of the Trinity

The demons did battle
The demons did fight
But they have no power
Against God's Holy Light

When night is its darkest
And all seems lost
The star from the Heavens
Will bring what you sought

Amen Amen Amen

The Warriors Among Us

God help Your children injured by war
The victims of darkness
The cries in the night
The nameless, the homeless
Those filled with fright

God help Your children
with wounds that won't heal
The blood and the conscious,
the flesh and the soul
The malignancies of darkness
That continue to grow

God help Your children
To see in the night
To conquer the darkness
To overcome fright

God teach Your children
To call Your Spirit near
To say Your Name
Your Holy Voice to hear

God save Your children
And stand before
The face of creation
The souls that would soar

God cleanse Your children
From darkness and sin
Forgive them and Bless them
And return to where we begin

Amen Amen Amen

As The Walls Of Hell Were Broken

Darkness built walls
To hide in the night
To imprison the victims
To perpetuate fright

Fear was the mortar
Greed was the steel
Power the stone
Before darkness it kneeled

The slaves of demons
Built the walls
The master of demons
Directed it all

The tears of the victims
The cries in the night
The master of demons
Perpetuated fright

God in His Mercy
God in His Might
Stood up to darkness
And conquered the night

Fire rained down
From Heaven above
The thunder of God
Motivated by Love

His children were victims
Of the darkness they called
They chose the demons
They built the walls

But God in His Mercy
And God with His Might
Stood up to darkness
And conquered the night

The demons fought
With all their might
To keep the victims
To perpetuate fright

As the walls tumbled
In shone the Light
God forgave His children
And dissolved their fright

And the thunder of Heaven
Unlocked the prison gates
Exposing the darkness
The guilt and the hate

God in His Mercy
God with His Might
Stood up to darkness
And conquered the night

Amen Amen Amen

The Time Of Angels Is At Hand

God sent a Heavenly Light into the darkness
Where no earthly light could fare
A Light to save His children
A Light to show God cares

And hope is on the horizon
For all who in darkness drown
For Heaven sent a King
Wearing a Holy Crown

He held the scales of justice
Mercy He did sound
This Holy King from Heaven
Wearing a Holy Crown

He stood before the darkness
He stands before this day
He holds a mirror of conscious
He is the Holy Way

He wears the Crown of Glory
The Lamb that Heaven sent
To fulfill the promises of Heaven
To teach us what was meant

When God in all His Glory
Told His children, who had gone
a stray
That He would send His Love
And show them a better Way

Amen Amen Amen

This World Is But A Battle Field
We Are So Long From Home
Lord Shield Us And Protect Us
With You We Are Never Alone
Amen
Amen
Amen

www.ingramcontent.com/pod-product-compliance
Lightning Source LLC
Chambersburg PA
CBHW051707040426
42446CB00008B/760